STAY STRONG!

AN ACTIVITY BOOK FOR YOUNG PEOPLE WHO ARE EXPERIENCING BULLYING

Kane Miller

A DIVISION OF EDC PUBLISHING

Kane Miller

A DIVISION OF EDC PUBLISHING

First American Edition 2019
Kane Miller, A Division of EDC Publishing

© 2018 Studio Press
Written by Dr. Sharie Coombes, Child, Family & Adult Psychotherapist,
Ed.D, MA (PsychPsych), DHypPsych(UK), Senior QHP, B.Ed.
Edited by Frankie Jones
Illustrated by Katie Abey
Designed by Rob Ward

First published in the UK in 2018 by Studio Press,
an imprint of Bonnier Books UK

For information contact:
Kane Miller, A Division of EDC Publishing
5402 S 122nd E Ave
Tulsa, OK 74146
www.kanemiller.com
www.myubam.com

Library of Congress Control Number: 2018942401

Printed in China
6 7 8 9 10

ISBN: 978-1-61067-862-9

STAY STRONG!

THIS BOOK BELONGS TO

_ _ _ _ _ _ _ _ _ _

WELCOME TO STAY STRONG!

Author
DR. SHARIE COOMBES
Child and Family Psychotherapist

We all feel overwhelmed from time to time. This fun activity book is a great way to get you thinking and talking about what is upsetting you, so you can get back to being you and enjoying life. The following pages show you how to cope with the way teasing and bullying make you feel, give you ideas about how to feel better and help you to find the courage to make it stop.

The activities help you to understand what is happening, feel stronger, make choices about how to react, talk to others about it (if you want to), and grow in confidence, independence and hopefulness. Use this book in a comfortable, safe place where you feel relaxed. It's up to you where you start, which pages you do and how often you come back to the pages you find most helpful. Do a page a day, if you like, or complete lots of pages at once. You make the rules!

Sometimes bullying and teasing make us feel really angry or hopeless and we believe that nothing will help, but there is ALWAYS a solution to every problem. Nothing is so big that it can't be sorted out or talked about, even if it feels that way right now. You could show some of these activities to important people in your life to explain how you're feeling and get help to stop the bullying. You can talk to an adult you trust at home or school to sort out the problems or ask an adult at home to take you to the doctor for some extra support.

It's normal to need a helping hand every now and then, and here are some organizations you can turn to if you don't want to talk to people you know. They've talked to thousands of children with every imaginable problem and will know how to help you.

KIDSAGAINSTBULLYING.ORG

An educational website designed for elementary school students to learn about what bullying is, how to respond and make it stop, what activities can help and how to take action in your community.

TEENSAGAINSTBULLYING.ORG

Created by and for teens, this website is a place for middle and high school students to find ways to address bullying, to take action, to be heard, and to own an important social cause.

CRISIS TEXT LINE

Serves anyone, in any type of crisis, providing access to free, 24/7 support.
Connect with a trained crisis counselor to receive free, 24/7 crisis support via text message. Text HELLO to 741741

www.crisistextline.org

NATIONAL SUICIDE PREVENTION LIFELINE

24/7, free and confidential support for people in distress. Call free or chat online. No matter what problems you're dealing with, whether or not you're thinking about suicide, if you need someone to lean on for emotional support or are worried about a friend or loved one call the Lifeline.
www.suicidepreventionlifeline.org
1-800-273-8255

DITCH THE LABEL

Ask anonymously for help with anything you're finding difficult.

www.ditchthelabel.org
Click the "I need help" section.

BOB'S JOB

History is full of people using their power to feel better about themselves by making others feel bad.

Animals also use this dominance behavior and fight to be leader of the pack or in the top dog's group.

Teasing is common and makes us feel powerless and unhappy if it continues or develops into bullying.

Bullying is the deliberate and repeated use of power by a person or group, in order to hurt or upset others.

People who like to hurt others want a reaction to show they've upset you, so the best defense is to be confident, positive, assertive, and resilient.

When there's no reaction, they move on.

PHYSICAL

Pushing or hurting you, damaging, hiding or stealing your belongings, using their body to scare you.

EMOTIONAL

Leaving you out, making you look silly, getting you into trouble, spreading rumors.

VERBAL

Name-calling, repeated teasing, mocking, insulting, or threatening.

CYBER

Using technology to bully, sending messages, sharing private chats, making threats, being offensive.

BULLYING HAS FOUR MAIN FORMS

When you've learned ways to stay strong and feel your own power, you can help others and make sure the adults around you step in when needed.

Bullying and teasing cause an ancient part of your brain, which we'll call "Bob," to freeze up and pump out chemicals, giving you unpleasant feelings in your body like fear, dread and frustration.

It's Bob's job to keep you safe, so he tries to get you to run away or fight.

BOB

THIS IS BOB.

Bob has an important job.

Bob sometimes freezes up.

Teach Bob to STAY STRONG.

Strong Bob, strong YOU!

He pops up in some activities.

Ready to start?

Look out for Bob.

Let's go!

Bob needs your help to learn to STAY STRONG by using this book.

COME BACK TO THIS PAGE ANYTIME YOU NEED TO.

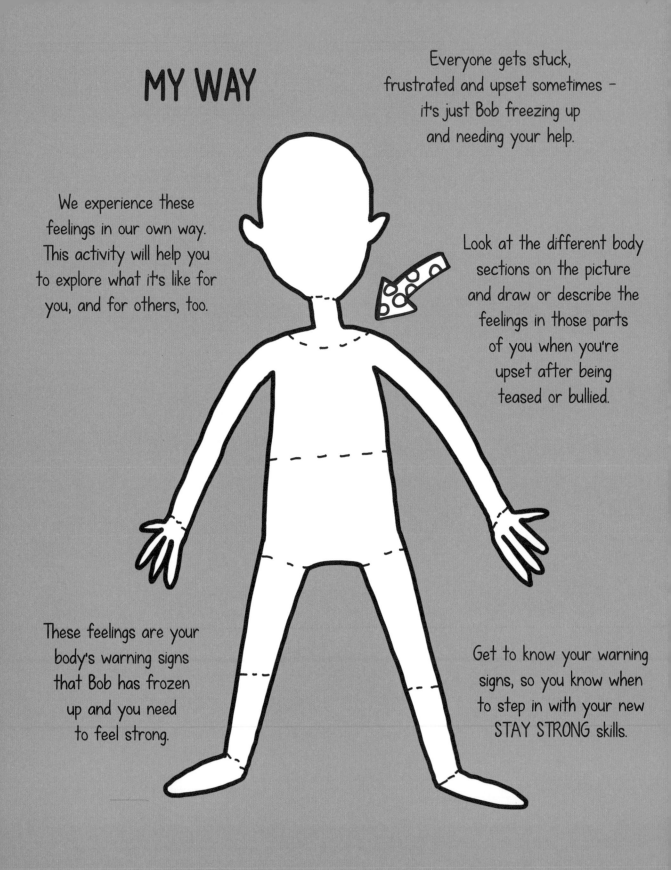

MY WAY

Everyone gets stuck, frustrated and upset sometimes – it's just Bob freezing up and needing your help.

We experience these feelings in our own way. This activity will help you to explore what it's like for you, and for others, too.

Look at the different body sections on the picture and draw or describe the feelings in those parts of you when you're upset after being teased or bullied.

These feelings are your body's warning signs that Bob has frozen up and you need to feel strong.

Get to know your warning signs, so you know when to step in with your new STAY STRONG skills.

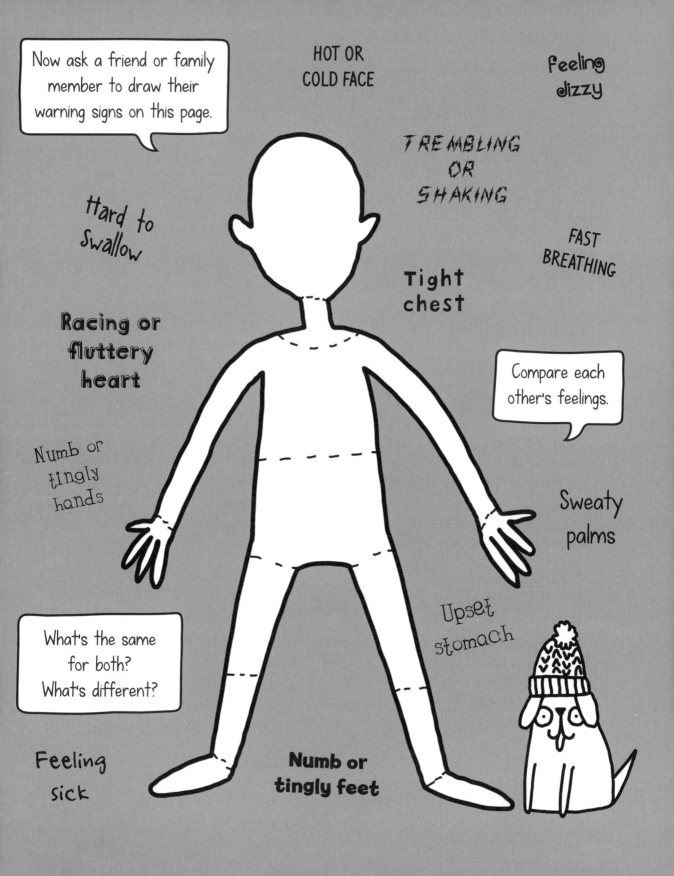

FEELING STRONG

No one feels strong all the time.
Your feelings matter and are part of you.
Get to know your feelings, so that you can quickly
recognize when you need help to STAY STRONG!

FRUSTRATED

Strong / Not Strong

DISGUSTED

Strong / Not Strong

Strong / Not Strong

Strong / Not Strong

ASHAMED

Strong / Not Strong

OVERWHELMED

Strong / Not Strong

Strong / Not Strong

COURAGEOUS

Strong / Not Strong

Strong / Not Strong

AFRAID

Strong / Not Strong

Strong / Not Strong

JOYFUL

Strong / Not Strong

Color and complete these pictures.
Check off the feelings you've had at different times and if
you felt strong or not strong when it happened.
Add your own ideas, too.

GUILTY

Strong / Not Strong

Strong / Not Strong

SURPRISED

Strong / Not Strong

COMFORTABLE

Strong / Not Strong

EMBARRASSED

Strong / Not Strong

Strong / Not Strong

JEALOUS

Strong / Not Strong

Strong / Not Strong

ANGRY

Strong / Not Strong

Do you have any of these feelings right now?
Why not add extra color or detail to the frames that really matter to you?
Come back and add to this page anytime you notice your feelings.

SELF-CONTROL

It's normal to feel upset when others make life difficult.

Draw yourself being strong, even when others are making you feel bad because they're being hurtful.

I CAN'T CONTROL THE BEHAVIOR OF OTHERS

I CAN CONTROL HOW I CHOOSE TO REACT

Color the words however you like.

Fill in these circles with frustrating memories of people being mean to you, teasing you or bullying you.

Come back to this page and add things as they happen.

CRUSH

When you understand your negative thoughts, they make more sense and it's easier to combat them.

Ready to start crushing those unhelpful beliefs?

LET'S DO IT!

Think something negative you believe about yourself and fill in this grid.

Make a fourth box here and write or draw about a time when it wasn't true.

SOMETHING NEGATIVE I BELIEVE ABOUT MYSELF	WHEN IT STARTED	WHAT HAPPENED TO CAUSE IT

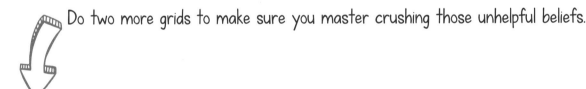

Do two more grids to make sure you master crushing those unhelpful beliefs.

SO MUCH MORE

These awards are for being who you are. Write your special qualities on or under the pictures and color them in.

When we feel we're not good enough, we give more power to the people who tease and bully us.

YOU ARE SO MUCH MORE THAN GOOD ENOUGH

KIND

FRIENDLY

MY SPECIAL QUALITIES

HARDWORKING

THOUGHTFUL

Imagine yourself being awarded each of these at a special ceremony.
Who is watching? Hear the loud cheers and applause you get.

MOUNTAIN OF STRENGTH

Some words just sound SO strong and can give you courage.

Fill these mountains with strong words and phrases that you love to read, write or hear that make you feel courageous and safe.

Why not say a couple of them to yourself the next time Bob freezes up?

I LOVE YOU

STRONG AS AN OX

POWERFUL

Write or draw about
a time when you
were strong.

TOUGH

HOME

STURDY

SOLID AS
A ROCK

YOU CAN DO IT

BREATHE STRONG, STAY STRONG

Finding your inner strength and calming Bob down can be easy when you learn to use your breathing to help you.

If you do this breathing exercise, others will automatically notice you're more assertive and confident without knowing why!

It's a secret weapon against being picked on.

3:5 BREATHING

This works wherever you are and whatever you're doing.

The best part is no one even knows you're doing it, so if you need to feel stronger without being noticed, give it a try.

If you're by yourself, you could close your eyes while you do it.

Get comfortable in a sitting position.

Notice your body breathing in and out.

After a few breaths, start to count along with yourself, making your "in" breath last for the count of three and your "out" breath last for the count of five, breathing smoothly.

Got it? Great! Keep going for as long you want to or until you feel OK again.

You can help to improve Bob's response if you get into the habit of practicing this every day for about five-to-ten minutes.

Try asking an adult to remind you every day or ask if they'll do it with you.

YOU'RE SO STRONG

Describe yourself using lots of positive words that begin with or use each of these letters.

Why not ask a friend to do it, too, on a piece of paper?

You could even describe each other and then read aloud your responses to give you both a confidence boost.

S
T
R
O
N
G

SASSY	SAFE	RELIABLE	NICE
SERIOUS	TIDY	RANDOM	GIGGLY
SPORTY	TRUSTWORTHY	OPTIMISTIC	GENEROUS

POWER-UP

If someone thinks they can have power over you, they might tease or try to bully you.

If you're easily upset or have trouble sticking up for yourself, this can make bullies feel even more powerful.

Sometimes others might pick on someone who's smarter than they are or different from them in some way.

Draw yourself feeling like you have no power.

Maybe you could add some words to describe how it feels.

Even superheroes know what it feels like to be teased or bullied.

The superheroes all found their power because they wanted things to change, and they now help other people change things, too.

Draw your inner superhero in full costume.

What's your power word that makes you change into your inner superhero?

Add words that people might say to your inner superhero to show you how much they admire you, and that make you feel powerful and strong.

SOCK IT TO 'EM

Write some powerful messages in these power bubbles.

SOME THINGS THAT WOULD
WORK WELL ARE:

I am smart.
I am just as
important as you.

I matter, too.
Stop!

When you've finished, shout each
one out loud into a mirror as
you punch the air in triumph!

STRONG COLORS

Color these mandalas in strong shades of greens, blues and purples.

FACE IT

Draw your face looking calm, confident and happy.

When you've finished your picture, think of a time someone was unkind to you and keep looking at your calm, confident and happy face until you can remember it without feeling upset.

GO WILD!

A group of zebras is called a

DAZZLE!

Decorate these individual zebras to show how dazzling and unique they are.

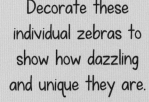

Think about their special qualities.
(Are they friendly?
Or maybe they're brave.)
Make each one stand out
from the crowd with bright
colors and vivid patterns.

UNDER THE SEA

Close your eyes for a moment and imagine yourself as a strong creature in a beautiful world under the sea.

Who is there with you?

Draw or write about your watery world below.

CATCH ME IF YOU CAN

Do something nice for someone and try not to get caught!

It only needs to be something small, like slipping them a friendly note, or making them something like a friendship bracelet or a card.

When you've done it, draw or write about it here and scale it out of five for how good it made you feel.

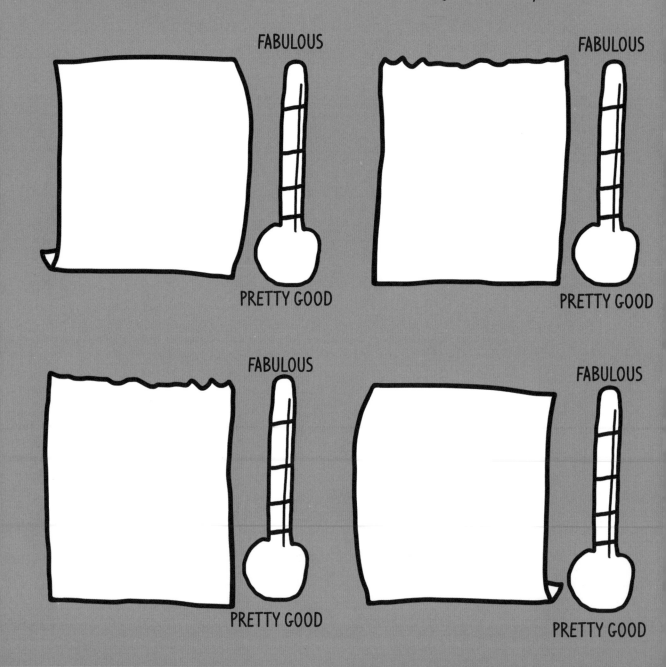

OTHER WAYS

When you feel under pressure, you might say things you shouldn't or wish you hadn't, or you might even take it out on someone else.

Use these speech bubbles to write the things you sometimes say when you're upset and then write what you could say instead.

Ask an adult for some
hand lotion with a lovely smell.

Find a friend or trusted adult you feel close
to who wants to do this activity with you.

SECOND SKIN

Spend five
minutes applying this
lotion all over their hands,
making sure you gently massage
it in really
well.

After five
minutes, swap and
get the other person to
massage the lotion into
your hands.

WARNING
Ask the adult to
make sure the lotion
is safe for you
to use.

NO BULLIES

Remember – it's never OK for someone to hurt you or your belongings.

Tell an adult if this happens to you.

When someone bullies, they're trying to feel better about themselves, be more popular, impress someone else or be seen as funny.

They aren't thinking about your feelings.

SOME IDEAS FOR YOU:

Stay calm

Walk away

Speak up

Stay strong

Don't fight

Don't get upset

Tell someone

Stand up for yourself

Use this page to make a poster of your own STAY STRONG rules.

Cut it out and stick it somewhere where you can see it to remind yourself every day.

STAY STRONG RULES

BEAT THE CLOCK

Choose something active that you enjoy doing and see how many times you can do it in two minutes.

It can be anything you want!

Ask an adult to set a timer and keep score if you want.

Practice every day for a week to see if you get quicker and can increase your score.

Record your results on the grid.

DAY 1	DAY 2	DAY 3	DAY 4	DAY 5	DAY 6	DAY 7

YOU DID IT! GO, YOU!

Why not make another grid and try again with another activity?

IDEAS:
Running in place
Singing a song
Drawing a shape
A clapping game
Bouncing a ball

STEP ASIDE

Your feelings come and go, but you're still the same person whether you're feeling strong or overwhelmed.

The great news is that you can make hurt feelings step aside and learn to feel strong again – it just takes practice.

I AM KIND.

I HAVE NICE MEMORIES.

Jot down here all the things about you that stay the same when you get overwhelmed.

Write down here all the feelings that can come and go.

ANGER

frustration

sadness

BOREDOM

HEART OF THE MATTER

Sometimes we upset other people even if we don't mean to. Everyone makes mistakes and says something hurtful every once in a while.

Saying sorry is a good way to put things right.

It makes others feel happy again, helps everyone to move forward and shows that you take responsibility for your action - even if it wasn't done on purpose.

Fill these hearts with "sorry" messages you weren't able to say at the time.

Come back and add more anytime you need to.

Maybe you could show your messages to the people they're meant for or even say sorry to their face?

Use some of the hearts for times when others should have said sorry to you but didn't. If you want, write down what they did.

STAY STRONG JAR

Find an empty jar with a lid.
Decorate it using pens or stickers.

Keep it somewhere where you can see it every day.

Make a label for it.

EVERY TIME YOU HAVE A LOVELY MEMORY, RECEIVE A COMPLIMENT, DO SOMETHING REALLY WELL OR FEEL POWERFUL, WRITE IT DOWN ON A SLIP OF PAPER OR A STICKY NOTE. FOLD IT AND PUT IT SAFELY IN THE JAR.

Whenever you need to power up, just grab your jar and read all the messages until you feel strong again.

SPEAK UP

It's good to speak your mind. Take some time to think about what you've been wanting to say. If you speak up for yourself, people won't pick on you.

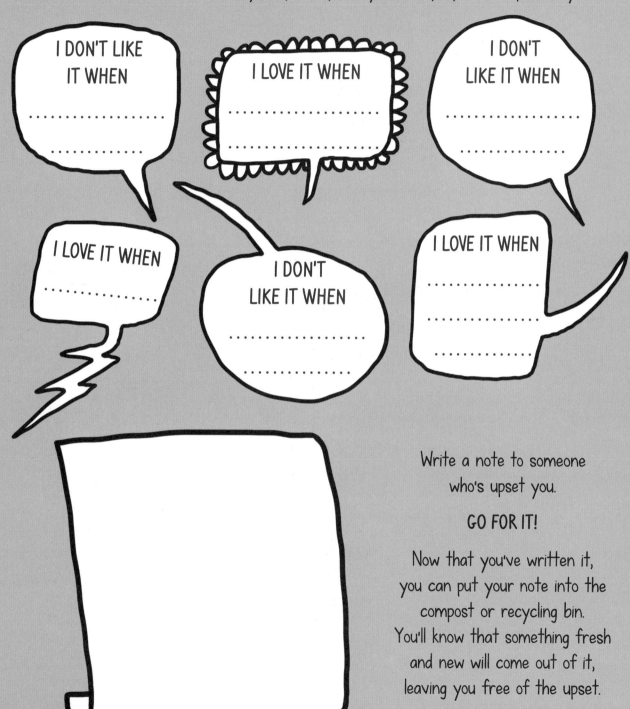

Write a note to someone who's upset you.

GO FOR IT!

Now that you've written it, you can put your note into the compost or recycling bin. You'll know that something fresh and new will come out of it, leaving you free of the upset.

BACK FROM THE FUTURE

Have you ever looked back on something and wished you'd had some good advice in a difficult moment?

Maybe you felt teased or bullied and could have used some support to STAY STRONG.

Dear Me,

Don't eat the apple.

Love,
Snow White
xx

Dear Me,

Remember the name Rumpelstiltskin.

Lots of love,
Queenie x

Write some postcards to yourself with inspiring messages and reminders that, once upon a time, might have been really useful.

CALL IT OUT

People who watch others being teased or bullied are

BYSTANDERS.

When bystanders don't call it out, this encourages more bullying.

UPSTANDERS

do call it out when people are teased or bullied.

They go out of their way to support people who've been upset.

CAN YOU BE AN UPSTANDER?

Make a list of things you can do to call bullying out.

Choose from the ideas on the checklist or think of your own, or both!

STAY STRONG
UPSTANDER CHECKLIST

Tell them to stop

Say positive things about people

Help someone who's hurt

Smile at someone who's sad

Stand up for someone who's being teased

Don't call anyone names

Be kind

Don't spread rumors

Tell an adult what you saw

Remember – one person CAN make the difference!

CHANGES

You know that caterpillars turn into butterflies.

Color in these gorgeous creatures
to make them stand out
from the crowd.

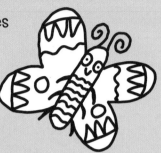

Fish spawn turns into shoals of shimmery fish.

Draw some other things that you know
change into something else as they get older.

HOW HAVE YOU ALREADY
CHANGED IN YOUR LIFE?

HOW ELSE MIGHT YOU
CHANGE IN THE FUTURE?

WHAT WILL YOU NEED TO DO OR HAVE,
FOR THESE CHANGES TO HAPPEN?

Draw or write
down your
thoughts.

ALL RIGHT, DUCK?

Ducks have waterproof feathers, so water just slides off them and they don't even get wet.

They stay strong, happy and calm, even in the rain.

Practice staying strong, happy and calm when you're upset – it really does work.

Get your ducks in a row and write or draw words, people or things that upset you pouring out of the buckets.

As you color them in, imagine hearing and watching them splash into the water without you even getting wet.

CYBER BULLYING

Nasty messages can be really upsetting and feel scary.

Everyone has things they don't like about themselves or that they feel ashamed of. Bullying makes these feelings grow and we feel like others know all our secrets.

They don't, it's just a trick of the mind because Bob is scared.

If you've received a mean message, write it down here and show it to someone you trust. Cover it with pictures or words to remind you how strong you are.

Remember, all social media sites have age limits.

HERE'S WHAT TO DO:

DON'T respond

SHOW the message to someone

BLOCK them

REPORT it

DELETE it

EVEN IF IT'S EMBARRASSING!

I-TIME

Make some time for a very special person – yes, that's you!

LET'S DANCE!

Play some music you love, and for the whole song, dance as though no one is watching.

Be as energetic or imaginative as you want.

You can do this on your own or with a friend.
If you're having fun, keep going with even more songs.

WITH COMPLIMENTS

Fill this page with compliments people have given you about your personality, actions, appearance, determination or skills.

It might be a teacher, a friend or a family member. Be sure to keep coming back and writing them down.

Color in segments of the power bank as your confidence grows, and keep coming back to read your compliments aloud to yourself. This will give you a boost until you're fully charged.

SHIELD ME

People sometimes make a mean comment and then say "just kidding!" or they'll tell you nobody likes you.

They know how much this will hurt because secretly they fear that no one likes them.

Try to remember that these comments say nothing about you but everything about them.

Fill your STAY STRONG shield with things or people that are special to you, to help you to cope under pressure.

The next time someone teases or bullies you, just picture your shield protecting you as you walk away and know that you are great!

A unicorn is strong and unique, just like you.

Color them in for extra STAY STRONG power!

FILL YOUR BOOTS

Fill these boots with all the things you love.

REASONS TO BE CHEERFUL

Write down one reason you have to be cheerful in each number and fill them in with color and patterns.

MEMORIES ARE MADE OF THIS

Think of a marvelous memory – maybe a day out, getting or giving a gift, going on vacation or a family celebration.

Chat to a friend or family member if you're stuck for an idea.

Make a movie of this memory in your mind and play it to yourself with your eyes closed.

Find your favorite scene from the movie, then draw it here and write down how it makes you feel.

Write down or draw things
you saw, heard, smelled,
touched or tasted.

WORTH A FORTUNE

This chatterbox game is a great way to let people know how much they mean to you or what you value most in them.

Write messages under the flaps that you'd love other people to read, or make it for yourself to remember how great you are, or choose a friend to do this with and write lovely things about each other.

YOU WILL NEED:

Piece of paper

Scissors*

Pens or crayons

TURN YOUR SHEET OF PAPER INTO A SQUARE

A. Fold the top corner down to make a triangle.

B. Cut off the spare rectangle under the triangle.

C. Unfold the triangle to get a square.

* Ask an adult to help you use the scissors.

1. Fold the paper square diagonally, making four identical triangles, then open it out.

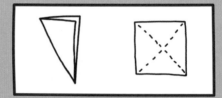

2. Fold each corner to the center of the sheet of paper to make a smaller square.

3. Turn it over and fold each corner to the center, making an even smaller square.

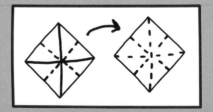 

4.	Fold your square in half both ways.

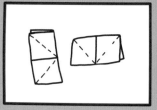

5.	Open the pockets behind each square and put your fingers into the spaces.

6.	Open and close each way just by moving your fingers!

Color the four outer squares in different colors.
Write a number from 1 to 8 on each of the eight inner triangles.
Behind each of these triangles, write a message of love.

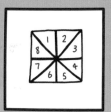
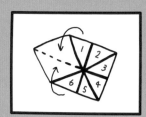
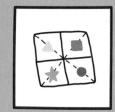

LET'S PLAY!

Ask a friend for a color from your four choices and spell it, opening the chatterbox once for each letter – R-E-D – open three times, one way, then the next.

Ask them to choose a number on display. Open the chatterbox this many times.

Ask for another number on display, lift up the flap and read your message!

HULLA-BALLOON

Color this picture in.

Do some 3:5 breathing as
you color and feel yourself
getting lighter than air
while you do it.

If you want to, write down the things that bother you on the
balloons and send them off into the sky, away from you forever.

FRESH AIR

Some people are like a breath of fresh air.

Fill these clouds however you like, with people who help you to breathe more easily by being helpful, kind, generous, supportive and other positive behaviors.

Why not finish your picture with a relaxing landscape and spend a few minutes imagining how comforting it is to be there?

TREASURE HUNT

Being in nature is one of the best ways to feel strong.

Go on a treasure hunt with a friend and take careful notice of the world around you.

Make a list like the one below on a piece of paper for everyone who's coming.

Check off each item when you see it. Remember to take your pencil!

PEBBLE	SPIDERWEB
LEAF	LITTER
FEATHER	SOMETHING ROUND
ACORN	
TWIG	SOMETHING LONG
PINE CONE	
RED LEAF	SOMETHING SPIKY
SEEDS	

Make sure an adult comes with you. Don't pick any plants or berries or go anywhere that's on private property.

THINK STRONG

Color in this poster to make it look strong.
Learn it by heart if you can.
Remembering to THINK before speaking will make sure that you don't upset others.

T
H   IS IT TRUE?
I   IS IT HELPFUL?
N   IS IT INSPIRING?
K   IS IT NECESSARY?

IS IT KIND?

Why not teach this to your friends, too?

MEAN MEANIE

When kind people are feeling bad about themselves, they can sometimes do or say mean things without stopping to think.

Is there a time when someone was mean to you?

Draw or write about what happened.

HOW DID YOU FEEL?

GRRRR

And what about a
time when you were
mean to someone else?

What happened?

HOW DO YOU THINK THE
OTHER PERSON FELT?

BREATHE, BE, BELIEVE

Do this breathing exercise anywhere, anytime.

It's perfect for finding your courage when you really need to.

No one needs to know you're doing it – they'll just sense you're feeling confident and strong.

It works like magic!

Sit or stand with a straight back and your arms relaxed.

1. BREATHE

BREATHE IN

Picture yourself being filled with powerful air and breathe in slowly, saying "BREATHE" in your head.

WRITE THE WORDS "BREATHE," "BE" AND "BELIEVE" IN THE THOUGHT BUBBLES.

TIP
Like all skills, it works better if you practice it every day in a quiet, calm place for a few minutes.

2. BE

HOLD YOUR BREATH

Picture yourself looking confident and hold your breath, saying "BE" in your head.

3. BELIEVE

BREATHE OUT

Picture yourself feeling really confident, then breathe out slowly, saying "BELIEVE" in your head.

You could picture a time you did something really well while you breathe out, saying "BELIEVE."

COLOR THIS IN

I BELIEVE IN ME

As you do this activity, remember all the times you've been strong, or imagine yourself facing up to someone and being able to stay strong because you believe in YOU!

This helps to teach Bob to stay strong more often.

LOVELY LETTER

Write a letter to someone who helped you out when you needed it.

Why were you grateful?
What difference did that person make?
What did you learn from it?

IT'S HARD TO ASK FOR HELP, BUT THE MORE YOU PRACTICE, THE EASIER IT GETS!

INSPIRATION STONES

Ask someone to take you to the beach, the woods or a park to find a few small and smooth pebbles.

You might find some in your backyard, too.

Wash your pebbles with dish soap and warm water. Dry them completely on paper towel.

Paint them or use permanent markers.

You could also leave them natural.

Write inspiring and strong words on them. Keep them on your desk or a shelf at home to remind you to stay strong.

If you find a piece of wood, you could glue them on as a little collection.

You can also make an inspiration wristband with words of your choice using paper.

Cover it in tape or plastic or laminate it. Tape it together at the join. Then you just have to look at your wrist for inspiration and confidence wherever you are.

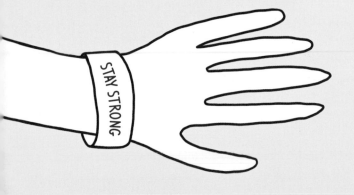

STRONG ARMS

A hug is a wonderful way to get Bob and you feeling strong.

Ask someone you trust for a hug right now.

Notice how it feels in your stomach.

If you can't hug someone you'd like to, close your eyes and imagine them hugging you.

See how it makes your stomach feel.

BODY LANGUAGE

Your body speaks loudly even when you say nothing at all. Others know how you're feeling by the way you hold your body.

Learn how to look strong and confident in a POWER POSE. Bob will recognize it and see that you're in control, which lets him know you're safe.

SAY "I CAN STAY STRONG" IN YOUR HEAD

SMILE

KEEP YOUR HEAD UP

MAKE EYE CONTACT

KEEP YOUR SHOULDERS BACK

HAVE BOTH FEET SQUARELY ON THE FLOOR

KEEP YOUR ARMS AND HANDS STILL

When you've practiced a few times, do it in front of the mirror and get used to seeing yourself like this.

Show an adult and ask them to guess how you're feeling when you do it.

List the places or people that make you feel less safe.
Remember to use your power pose in these places or when
you are with these people the next time you come across them.

PLACES

PEOPLE

DRAW YOUR POWER POSE.

You could even draw a
protective bubble around
yourself to make sure you
feel able to STAY STRONG.

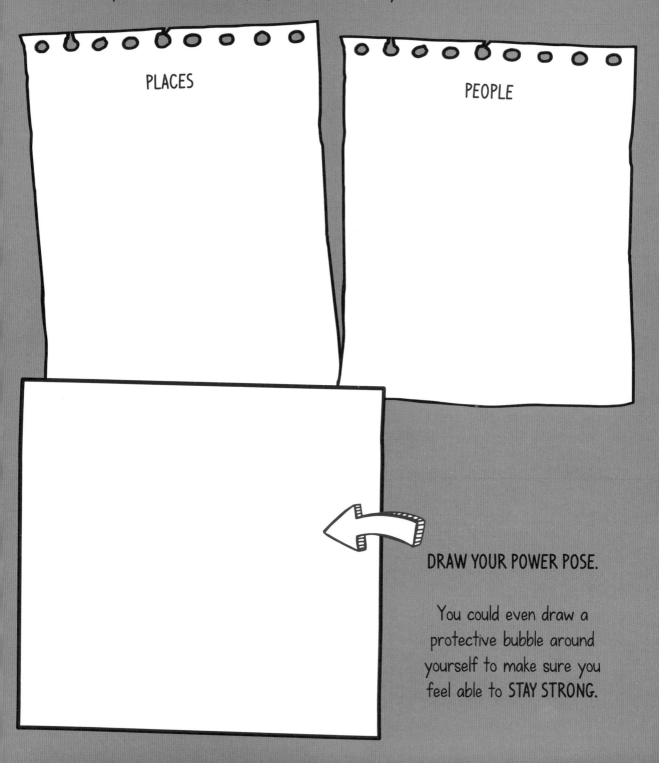

Choose a few friends and family members, and write or draw what you like about them.

KNOWING YOU

KNOWING ME

Now find out what they like about you.

You could ask them to fill in this page or you can do it yourself after asking them what they like about you.

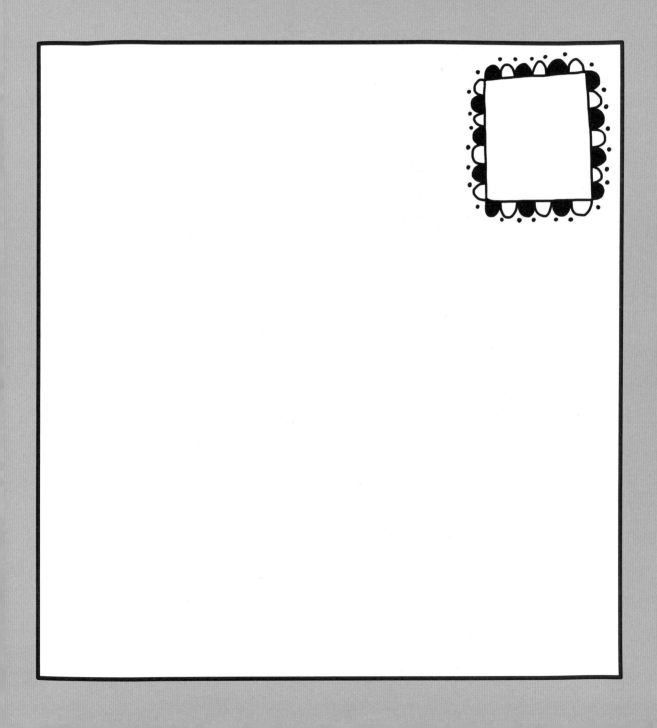

GETTING ON FAMOUSLY

Think of someone famous either from history or the present day whom you really admire.

Draw your person or glue a picture of them here.

What qualities does this person have that especially impress you?

What encouraging message would they give you when you're feeling overwhelmed?

Write it down in the bubble and imagine hearing them say it to you.

Keep coming back to hear this message anytime it's needed.

WEEK NOT WEAK

Write down all the things you did well this week.

Write down who noticed what you did well – even if it's you who noticed. You're important, too!

DATE	WHAT I DID WELL	WHO NOTICED

TALENT SCOUT

Be an undercover talent scout.

Your mission, should you choose to accept it, is to find all your own hidden talents.

BE A SUPER SLEUTH!

Keep watching, listening, and noticing.

You never know when something really special might pop up and surprise you.

You could recruit some family and friends to be scouts to help you out.

When you find one of your talents, write about it or draw it in a magnifying glass. Keep coming back until you've filled them all.

HOW WILL YOU GROW YOUR TALENTS?

YOU'VE GOT THE POWER!

You've got the power to change what you believe about yourself and how you feel.

Try using your power on two of your own negative beliefs by using these machines. Now, when someone else makes you feel bad, you know what to do to change how you feel!

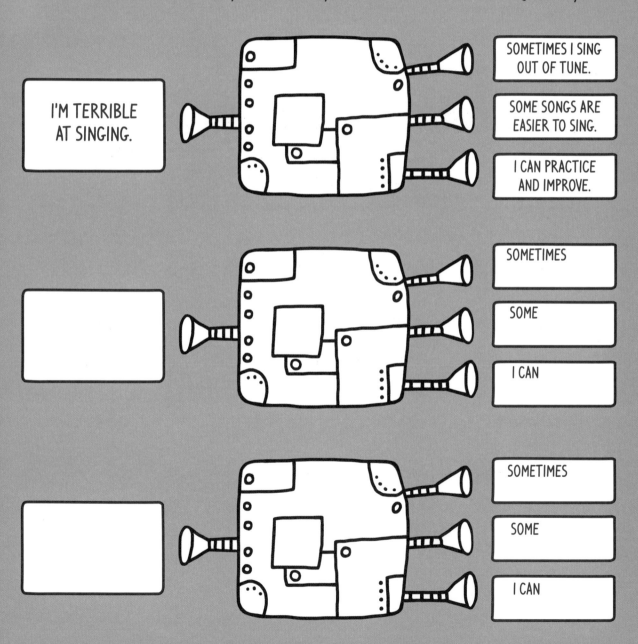

I'M TERRIBLE AT SINGING.

SOMETIMES I SING OUT OF TUNE.

SOME SONGS ARE EASIER TO SING.

I CAN PRACTICE AND IMPROVE.

SOMETIMES

SOME

I CAN

SOMETIMES

SOME

I CAN

STAY STRONG BOX

Make yourself a box of goodies to give you a bit of help when things are feeling like too much.

To make your Stay Strong Box, find a shoebox and decorate it so it's special to you. You can even use an ice cream carton, gift box or gift bag. Find things that will help you to stay strong when you need to.

It doesn't matter what you choose as long as you like looking at it or feeling it in your hands.

SOME IDEAS YOU MIGHT FIND HELPFUL

SMALL MIRROR FOR MAKING FACES AT YOURSELF

PIECE OF FABRIC WITH YOUR FAVORITE SCENT SPRAYED ON IT

BOTTLE OF BUBBLES

THIS BOOK

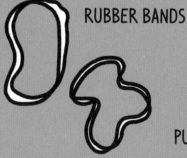

PHOTO OF SOMEONE YOU LOVE

BUBBLE WRAP

FIDGET TOY

YOUR FAVORITE COLLECTOR CARD OR TOY

SILLY PUTTY OR SLIME

HIGHLIGHTERS

RUBBER BANDS

PIPE CLEANERS

PUZZLE BOOK

SMELLY PENS

SAY WHAT NOW?

What would you say to a friend who is feeling down?

Try coming up with thoughtful and supportive responses in the boxes.

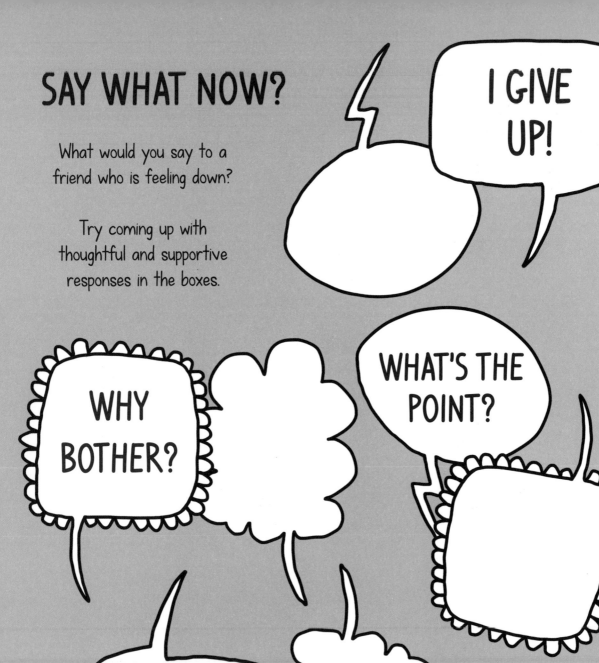

I GIVE UP!

WHY BOTHER?

WHAT'S THE POINT?

NOTHING I SAY OR DO WILL MATTER ANYWAY.

Imagine what you'd like to hear to be able to STAY STRONG if it was you feeling bad.

YOU MAKE ME FEEL...

Think of a person or situation.

Scale how strong you feel when you are around them or dealing with it.

One is not at all strong, five is quite strong and ten is superstrong.
You can decide what the numbers in between mean.

What do you need to do to move up two places on the scale?

What help do you need to move up four places?

DO THIS WITH TWO PEOPLE OR SITUATIONS.

PERSON OR SITUATION:

....

....

SCALE OF HOW YOU FEEL:

....

HOW WOULD YOU MOVE TWO PLACES?

....

....

....

HOW WOULD YOU MOVE FOUR PLACES?

....

....

....

PERSON OR SITUATION:

....

....

SCALE OF HOW YOU FEEL:

....

HOW WOULD YOU MOVE TWO PLACES?

....

....

....

HOW WOULD YOU MOVE FOUR PLACES?

....

....

....

10
9
8
7
6
5
4
3
2
1

I'LL BE THERE

Think of all the people whom you can rely on to support you when you need a helping hand.

Write their names on this helping hand to remind you and then decorate it however you like.

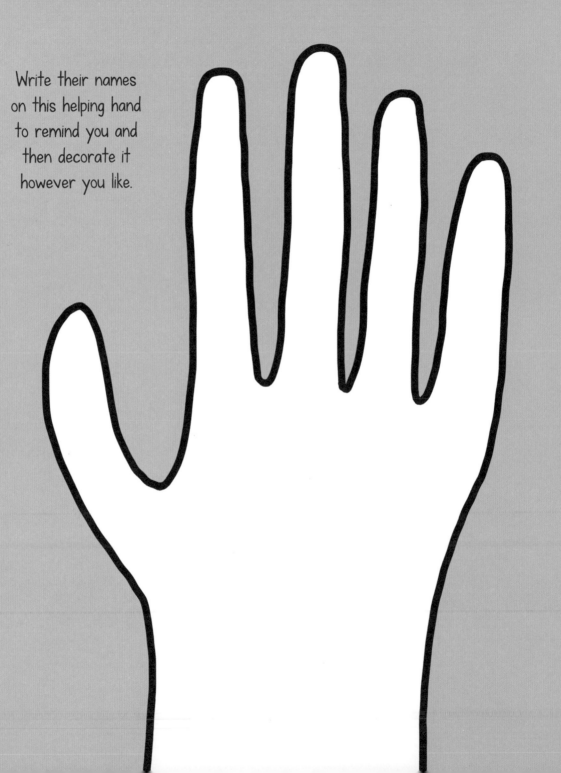

SAFE ZONE

Find a calm, quiet place to do this activity.

Draw somewhere where you feel completely safe, relaxed and calm.

You could even stick in a photo or picture from a magazine.

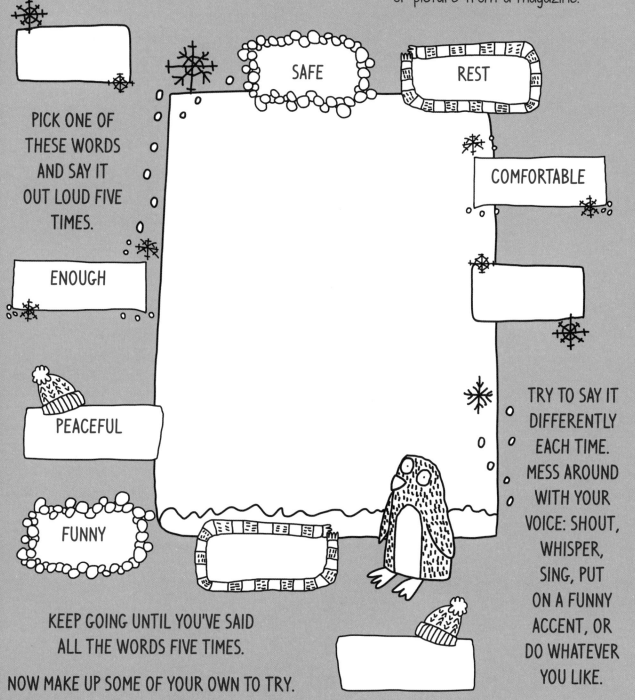

PICK ONE OF THESE WORDS AND SAY IT OUT LOUD FIVE TIMES.

SAFE

REST

COMFORTABLE

ENOUGH

PEACEFUL

FUNNY

TRY TO SAY IT DIFFERENTLY EACH TIME. MESS AROUND WITH YOUR VOICE: SHOUT, WHISPER, SING, PUT ON A FUNNY ACCENT, OR DO WHATEVER YOU LIKE.

KEEP GOING UNTIL YOU'VE SAID ALL THE WORDS FIVE TIMES.

NOW MAKE UP SOME OF YOUR OWN TO TRY.

STRONG WARRIOR

Other people sense what we believe about ourselves and don't usually tease or bully anyone strong or confident.

The beliefs that grow are the ones you feed.
Let's feed your strong inner warrior!

Try this by yourself or with an adult or friend so you can take turns to read the instructions aloud.

WARRIOR 1 POSE — I AM STRONG

Stand straight, feet together, arms out at your sides.

Step forward and bend your front knee, with your back leg straight out behind you. Arch your back, stretching your arms and hands up to the sky. Look straight ahead with a powerful expression on your face.

Take a deep breath in for a count of three.
As you breathe out, say aloud "I AM STRONG."
Let all the breath go.
Stay in the pose and do this four more times.

Breathe normally, bringing your arms back down to your sides and your feet back together with straight legs. Switch legs and repeat.

WARRIOR 2 POSE — I AM POWERFUL

From Warrior 1, stretch your arms out in front of you.

Turn your chest, bringing one arm out to the front, with the other stretched behind you.

Look straight ahead with a powerful expression on your face.

Take a deep breath in for a count of three.

As you breathe out, say aloud "I AM POWERFUL."

Let all the breath go.

Stay in the pose and do this four more times.

Breathe normally, turning your chest the other way and gliding your arms around, so they switch positions. Repeat.

WARRIOR 3 POSE — I AM IMPORTANT

From Warrior 2, bring both arms in front of you.

Straighten your front leg and lift your back foot off the ground a little.

Open your arms wider for balance if needed.

Look straight ahead with a powerful expression on your face.

Take a deep breath in for a count of three.

As you breathe out, say aloud "I AM IMPORTANT."

Let all the breath go.

Stay in the pose and do this four more times.

Breathe normally, bringing your arms down to your sides, with your feet back together and straight legs. Switch legs and repeat.

Put your hands together, smile and stand in Mountain Pose breathing calmly for a little while.

YES I CAN

CAN YOU STAY STRONG?

Think of the many ways you can stay strong and all the things you can do.

Write down or draw these all over this page.

Have you ever tried looking confident with your body and face and saying "you're right" when someone is mean? It can be a powerful way to stop teasing.

You can avoid win/lose situations by being able to STAY STRONG.

HOPES

What exciting things would you like to do in your life?

THINK BIG!

Stay strong and you'll do it.

CHEERLEADERS

Is there a particular goal you want to achieve?

Maybe something you want to do tomorrow, next week, next month, next year, or even further away.

It can be something little or something amazing.

Who will be there cheering you on?

What will they say when you get there?

What will they be saying to encourage you?

LEARN TO FLY

DESIGN A LIFESAVING DEVICE

Can you think of a chant they might repeat to keep you going?

BECOME A
SCIENTIST

What do their banners say?

What will you say
when you make it?

GET MY
BLACK BELT

SAIL AROUND
THE WORLD

BIG UP

When we feel overwhelmed, things often seem much bigger than they really are. This activity will help you when there's something taking up all your thoughts.

What's feeling huge for you at the moment?

What are the three most important parts of this problem?

List what you can do to get it sorted out and out of your way for good.

Remember, you don't have to do it all by yourself – add who can help with the different parts.

Here are some top tips to help you deal with huge thoughts –
there's some space for you to add your own as well.

GET PLENTY OF SLEEP

DRINK PLENTY OF WATER

EAT HEALTHILY

MAKE A LIST

FOCUS ON WHAT'S
IMPORTANT

TELL SOMEONE

DREAM TEAM

Getting great sleep means you can stay strong during the day. Bob needs sleep!

HERE ARE SOME THINGS YOU MIGHT NEED FOR A GOOD NIGHT:

A DRINK

READ A BEDTIME STORY

A HUG

LISTEN TO SOMETHING RELAXING

WARM SOCKS

FAVORITE TEDDY

NIGHT-LIGHT

QUIET

Make your own personal list of what YOU need in order to sleep tight.

Draw yourself tucked up all cozy and sleeping calmly all night long.

HAPPY SNAP

Remember to say who they are and why or how they are like you.

Illustrate these playing cards with famous people
or people you know who are just like you in some way.

Use magazine pictures if you prefer.

MOLLIE

LIKES FISH

THE PAGE FOR GROWN-UPS

This activity book is perfect for parents, teachers, learning mentors, social workers, therapists, and youth leaders who want to help children to stay strong when dealing with teasing and bullying.

Modern life in a society that promotes perfection, popularity and success is stressful, and can cause children to experience many internal and external pressures. Comparing themselves with others affects their confidence, while bullying and teasing can make them feel vulnerable and believe they aren't good enough. When this happens, children may get overwhelmed or develop a sense of hopelessness and helplessness and struggle to cope, because they don't have the life experience or language to explain their distress. You might notice a decline in self-esteem and more angry or sad outbursts, stomachaches, headaches, or tiredness, as well as avoidance of previously enjoyed places, people, and activities.

In a loving and nurturing environment, children are resilient and will often work through problems without needing additional help. This book enables the child to combat negative thoughts, explore, express, and explain feelings, and open up the conversation with you. The fun activities build vital self-confidence and assertiveness, improve understanding of emotions, and encourage the capacity for inner strength, appropriate self-reliance, and hopefulness.

If your child's distress or fear persists beyond three months or escalates rather than decreases, you can talk to their school, a doctor or a counselor.

DR. SHARIE COOMBES

CHALLENGE THE STORM™

Sharing stories, resources and support for people facing emotional challenges.

Share your story and express yourself openly, and free from judgement.

www.challengethestorm.org

NATIONAL PARENT HELPLINE

Support and resources for parents worried about their children.

www.nationalparenthelpline.org

Tel: 1-855- 4A PARENT
1-855-427-2736

STOPBULLYING.GOV

An official website of the United States government. Support for parents and school staff worried about bullying.

NATIONAL ALLIANCE ON MENTAL ILLNESS (NAMI)

Educate, advocate, listen, lead.

The NAMI HelpLine can be reached Monday through Friday, 10 am-6 pm.

NAMI is the nation's largest grassroots mental health organization dedicated to building better lives for the millions of Americans affected by mental illness.

www.nami.org

Tel: 1-800-950-NAMI (6264)
info@nami.org

GOODTHERAPY.ORG®

Helping people find therapists. Advocating for ethical therapy.

GoodTherapy.org offers a directory to help you in your search for a therapist. Using the directory, you can search by therapist location, specialization, gender, and age group treated. If you search by location, your results will include the therapists near you and will display their credentials, location, and the issues they treat.

Tel: 1-888-563-2112 ext. 1
www.goodtherapy.org